A Life of Love

A Life of Love

The Story of

Elizabeth Barrett Browning

by

Mary Logue

Illustrated by

Peter Kavanagh

The Child's World®

Library of Congress Cataloging-in-Publication Data
Logue, Mary.
Elizabeth Barrett Browning: love / Logue, Mary.
p. cm.
Summary: Traces the life of the gentle English poet, with an emphasis
on the value of love in her experiences.

ISBN 1-56766-225-0

1. Browning, Elizabeth Barrett, 1806-1861--Juvenile literature.
2. Women poets, English--19th century-- Biography--Juvenile literature.
3. Love--Juvenile literature.
[1. Browning, Elizabeth Barrett 1806-1861. 2. Women--Biography.]
I. Title. II. Series.
PR4193.L64 1996
821'.8--DC20
95-44422
AC

Contents

The Barrett Family

One day, when Elizabeth Barrett was ten years old, she wrote a story. As she worked on it, her brothers and sister were all around her. Some of them were studying Latin. Her younger sister was banging away on the piano.

Mrs. Barrett taught all of her children at home. That was not unusual in 1816.

When Elizabeth finished her story, she gave it to her mother. She was very proud of it.

"Mother," she said, "I want you to write copies to be sold to the public."

Mrs. Barrett laughed. At that time, there were no copy machines. She would have had to write out each copy by hand!

That was the start of Elizabeth's writing career.

Elizabeth Barrett lived in the English countryside. She was the oldest child in the Barrett family. She had 11 brothers and sisters—three girls and eight boys. They were a very close and happy family. They had lots of room on their estate, so Elizabeth kept a whole zoo of animals. She even tamed a squirrel and had her own pony.

Elizabeth learned the importance of love from her family. Her parents were deeply in love with each other. They also showered their children with affection.

Coming from such a tight-knit family, Elizabeth wrote often of love. Little did she know that one day, she would write one of the most famous love poems in the world.

What is *Love?*

*L*ove is a strong feeling of affection for someone else. Often, you love people who are close to you, like your parents and your brothers and sisters. When you have really good friends, you might love them too.

You can also like something so much that you say you love it. Many children love dogs or love horses or love to go swimming. Some, like Elizabeth, love to read.

Teenage Years

Elizabeth's father, Edward Barrett, published her first book when she was 14. It was a long poem called *The Battle of Marathon*.

When she saw the book, Elizabeth was ecstatic. She called writing "the very soul of my being."

The next year, she fell ill. The doctors didn't know what was wrong with her. Perhaps, they thought, something was wrong with her spine. Or perhaps she had eaten something that was bad for her. She stayed sick for more than a year. She had to live away from her family so a doctor could watch over her.

She had to stay in bed. It was a very unhappy year for Elizabeth.

When she returned home, she was still quite weak. It took her years to regain her strength. But when she did, she started writing again.

This time she wrote a book of poetry called *An Essay on the Mind*.

One night, the Barrett family was sitting down to dinner. Suddenly, there was a knock on the door. A package had arrived. It was Elizabeth's new book.

Everything stopped while Elizabeth's father opened up the package and they all saw the book for the first time. Everyone read it, even her younger brothers and sisters.

Her mother said how pleased both she and Elizabeth's father were, calling Elizabeth "our beloved child."

I love my own dear land—it doth rejoice
The soul, to stretch my arms, and lift my voice,
To tell her of my love! I love her green
And bowery woods, her hills in mossy sheen . . .

This is part of a poem by Elizabeth Barrett Browning. She wrote it when she was 20 years old. She was writing of her love for her country, England.

First Love

At 21, Elizabeth Barrett was happy with her life. In the morning, she would stay in bed and read. Later, she would take leisurely walks on the family estate. And, of course, she worked on her poems. She was a small woman, with thick brown hair and large brown eyes.

Barrett did not have any boyfriends. She was too shy and never very healthy. She stayed at home and worked on her writing.

One day an older, married gentleman, Hugh Stuart Boyd, wrote and told her how much he had enjoyed *An Essay on the Mind*. They wrote letters back and forth. Boyd, who had gone blind in his 30s, was a scholar and a writer. He and Elizabeth had many things in common.

In the 1800s, people communicated by writing letters. They had no TV, no radio, and no telephone. If they wanted to invite friends over for dinner, they wrote them a letter. Finally, after many letters, Barrett went to visit Boyd.

They became close friends. She went every week to read books to him and to talk about poetry. When Barrett's mother died, Boyd became even more important to her. He was able to pull her out of her despair. He encouraged her to keep writing.

But after a while, her relationship with Boyd changed. She fell in love with him. Sometimes we fall in love with people who don't—or can't—love us back. Boyd was old enough to be Barrett's father, and he had a wife. He was not a good person for her to fall in love with.

Boyd moved away. When Barrett saw him again a few years later, she was over her crush. She saw many things she didn't like about him. For example, he only thought about himself. He didn't really care about other people.

So ended her first love.

London Life

In 1836, the Barrett family moved to London, one of the most important cities in the world. In London, there were always parties to go to and plays to see and people to visit. Elizabeth Barrett was glad to live there, because she could meet other writers.

Soon after they moved to London, a good friend of Barrett's took her to a party. There she met a writer, Mary Mitford. Mitford was nearly 60. She wrote books about living in the country. She was warm and full of energy. She and Barrett would be friends for the rest of their lives.

Mitford gave Barrett a book of poems by a man named Robert Browning. Barrett read the poems. She found them very powerful. They made her think. She decided that Robert Browning was one of her favorite poets. She wondered what he was like as a person.

She worked hard on a new book of poetry. She wrote a long poem called *The Seraphim*. A *seraphim* is an angel. Her father liked the poem, and it was published in 1838. This was her first book to receive much attention. Many people liked it. A newspaper called her "a genuine poetess." Barrett was very pleased. She had an exciting new life in a new town with good friends.

I am swift, I am strong,
The love is bearing me along.

This is said by one of the angels in the poem, *The Seraphim*. As he is flying, he says that it is *love* that is holding him up.

A Sad Three Years

Now came one of the saddest times in Elizabeth Barrett's life. She fell very ill again. She had a bad cough all winter. That next summer, she didn't get better. Doctors came to see her, but they had no medicines to help her. All they could do was send her to a warmer climate.

Elizabeth went to stay in a small town on the coast of England. Her favorite brother, Bro, went with her. Even with his company, her life there was very boring. The doctor told her not to work. There was nothing else to do. She rested in bed and wrote letters and read magazines. She stayed there for nearly three years.

Only Bro could keep her amused. He told her jokes and brought her little presents to cheer her up. He talked with her for hours.

One fine summer day, Bro went sailing with three other men. The sea was calm, but their boat tipped over and they all drowned.

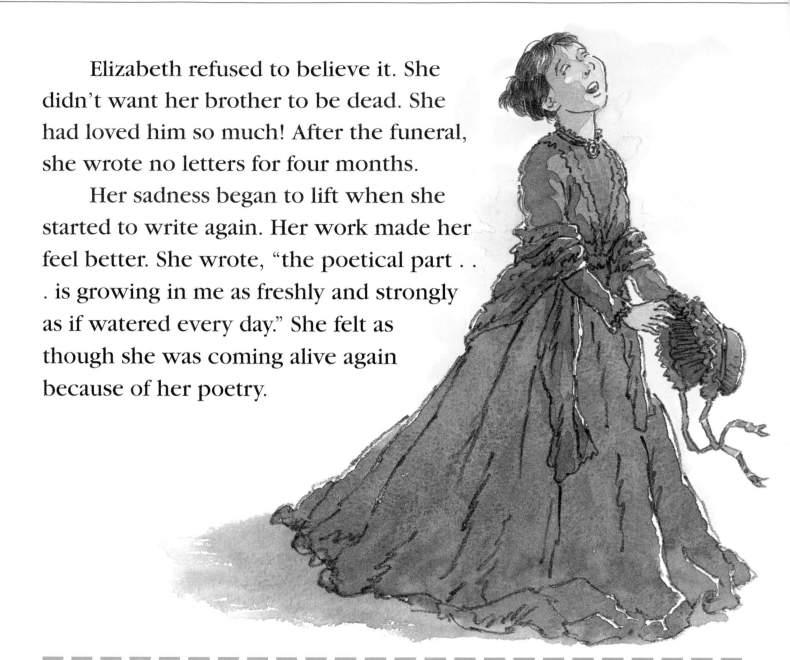

Elizabeth refused to believe it. She didn't want her brother to be dead. She had loved him so much! After the funeral, she wrote no letters for four months.

Her sadness began to lift when she started to write again. Her work made her feel better. She wrote, "the poetical part . . . is growing in me as freshly and strongly as if watered every day." She felt as though she was coming alive again because of her poetry.

*L*ove can bring joy to your life. But it can also bring sorrow. When people we love die, we often miss them for a long time. We miss them because we loved them.

Flush

With Bro gone, Elizabeth Barrett felt very alone. When she went back to London, her good friend Mary Mitford said, "My dog has just had puppies. You should take one."

But Barrett wasn't sure. She told Mitford, "Your puppies are too valuable. I couldn't just take one."

But Mitford insisted.

Finally, Barrett accepted the puppy. The golden cocker spaniel came to live with her when he was six months old. She named him Flush. Barrett adored her dog. Her letters to Mary Mitford were all about him.

Her family was delighted to see her so happy. They gave Flush whatever he wanted. Flush liked his toast buttered, so they buttered it. He didn't like mutton, so they gave him beef. Flush didn't like to be alone, so someone always had to stay with him. Barrett wrote in a letter, "Flush is spoilt!"

Flush loved Barrett more than anyone else. He even slept in her bed. The doctor told her Flush had to have a bath if he was going to sleep in her bed! So Flush was bathed every day. He rarely moved from Barrett's side. The dog's love did what no one else could—it made Barrett smile and laugh again.

Flush lived with Barrett for 14 years. He was "dognapped" three times. In London, people sometimes stole dogs. Then they would tell the owners that for a certain price they could get their dogs back. Barrett always paid to get her dog back. Once, she even went herself to fetch him.

She loved him so much, she wrote a poem about him. It's called *To Flush, My Dog*. In it she describes the joy of owning her dog.

Elizabeth described the way her dog, Flush, would behave:

Leap! thy broad tail waves a light,
Leap! thy slender feet are bright,
Canopied in fringes;
Leap! those tasseled ears of thine
Flicker strangely, fair and fine
Down their golden inches.

A Magic Meeting

Barrett had never stopped thinking about her favorite poet, Robert Browning. She wrote a love ballad called "Lady Geraldine's Courtship." In it she paid compliments to Browning's work. When her poem was published, she hoped he would see it.

A few months later, Robert Browning sat down and wrote her a letter. He was flattered that she had written about him. He was a younger poet and not as well known as Barrett.

Browning's letter to her was very warm and friendly. He told her he loved poetry with all his heart. She wrote back to him. She asked him to tell her what he liked and did not like about her poetry.

Their letters grew longer and more friendly. They told each other a lot about themselves. Barrett was delighted with the letters. But Browning wanted to meet her. He asked her many times, but she refused.

IIc was puzzled. Why didn't she want to meet him? He finally realized why. She was afraid he wouldn't like her as much in person.

Barrett finally gave in and said he could come to her family's house on Wimpole Street. Browning was curious about her, but very confident. Barrett felt quite differently. She lay on her couch and waited. She acted as if something horrible were going to happen.

When Browning walked into the room, he moved quickly to hold her hand. He was a small man, but he had lots of energy. He spoke with a loud voice and had strong opinions on everything. Barrett relaxed. She liked him immensely.

They saw each other weekly for a year. They fell in love. During their courtship, Barrett wrote a series of love poems for Browning called *Sonnets from the Portuguese*. She showed them to no one.

I should not love withal, unless that thou
Hadst set me an example, shown me how,
When first thine earnest eyes with mine were crossed,
And love called love.

This is a poem Barrett wrote to Robert Browning, Sonnet 12 of *Sonnets from the Portuguese*. In it, she tells Browning that he taught her how to love him.

Marriage, a Child

On a quiet Saturday morning, Elizabeth Barrett walked to a church with her maid. There she met Robert Browning and his cousin. A minister was waiting. Elizabeth and Robert were married in a very simple ceremony, and she became Elizabeth Barrett Browning.

A week later, they moved to Italy. The happiest time of Elizabeth's life had begun.

Elizabeth and Robert were very much in love. They found more and more to like about each other. Elizabeth wrote to her sister, "I am as happy as any one ever was in the world . . . If we ever quarrel you may expect it to snow stars."

At the age of 43, Elizabeth had a son. Another important person had entered her life. She loved her new son, Pen, very much.

The Brownings went up into the mountains to escape Italy's summer heat. One warm day out on their patio, Elizabeth slipped some papers into Robert's hands.

Robert sat down and read what she had given him. He couldn't believe his eyes. Elizabeth had written 43 poems about her love for him. He thought they were the best poems she had ever written. He wanted her to publish them.

He later wrote, "I dared not reserve to myself the finest Sonnets written in any language since Shakespeare."

Sonnets from the Portuguese was published in England in 1847 and became her best-known work.

Elizabeth Barrett Browning lived for another 12 years. She was 55 when she died. She had based her life on the love she felt for others—her father, her brothers and sisters, her friends, her child, and most importantly, her husband, Robert.

Writing poetry during her final years, Elizabeth expressed her love through her poetry.

Today, her poems are used by other people to express their love. When they want to tell someone how much they love them, they send a poem by Elizabeth Barrett Browning.

Her words of love live on today.

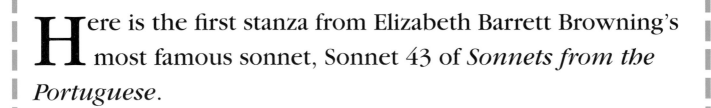

Here is the first stanza from Elizabeth Barrett Browning's most famous sonnet, Sonnet 43 of *Sonnets from the Portuguese*.

How do I love thee? Let me count the ways.
I love thee to the depth and breadth and height
My soul can reach, when feeling out of sight
For the ends of Being and ideal Grace.

Study Guide

1. Make a list of people you love.

Make a list of things you love to do.

2. In a poem, Elizabeth wrote, "The love is bearing me along." She meant that love gave her support. How did love do that in her own life?

3. When Elizabeth's brother died, she felt sad. What happens when something—or someone—you love goes away?

4. Elizabeth Barrett Browning's most famous poem begins, "How do I love thee? Let me count the ways." Is it really possible to count how many ways we love someone?

Study Guide Answers

1. It is important, from time to time, to see how many people and things you love. It is good to realize how important love is in your life. You probably love everyone in your family. Sometimes you might be mad at a brother or sister, but that does not mean you do not love them.

2. Love helped Elizabeth get through some of the difficult times in her life. Her whole family always supported and encouraged her. Her brothers and sisters helped her when she was sick. Her dog made her laugh when she was sad. And her husband, Robert Browning, taught her what true love was. He inspired many of her poems.

3. When something—or someone—we love dies or leaves, it leaves a hole in our life. Because we loved them, we miss them. No one will ever replace them! But our lives go on. The world is filled with people and things for us to love.

4. We cannot actually count the ways we love someone. And that is what the poem is really about. The poem says it is impossible to count such a thing. Browning is almost making fun of herself for trying to write about all the different ways she loves her husband.

Elizabeth Barrett Browning Time Line

1806 Elizabeth Barrett is born.

1820 Barrett publishes her poem *The Battle of Marathon*.

1826 Elizabeth writes *An Essay on the Mind*.

1836 Barrett and her family move to London. She meets Mary Mitford and reads poems by Robert Browning.

1838 Barrett publishes *The Seraphim*.

1846 Robert Browning and Elizabeth are married in London.

1847 Elizabeth publishes her *Sonnets from the Portuguese*.

1861 Elizabeth Barrett Browning dies in Italy.